A Sunny Day

by Robin Nelson

first step nonfiction

It is a sunny day!

The sunshine feels warm.

When it is sunny,
the sky is blue.

It is bright outside.

When it is sunny,
ice cream **melts.**

Flowers open.

When it is sunny,
skin can **burn.**

We see our **shadows.**

When it is sunny,
we sit in the **shade.**

We wear sunglasses.

When it is sunny,
we have a picnic.

We go for a walk.

When it is sunny, we run
through a sprinkler.

We go swimming.

When it is sunny,
we play with friends.

A sunny day is fun!

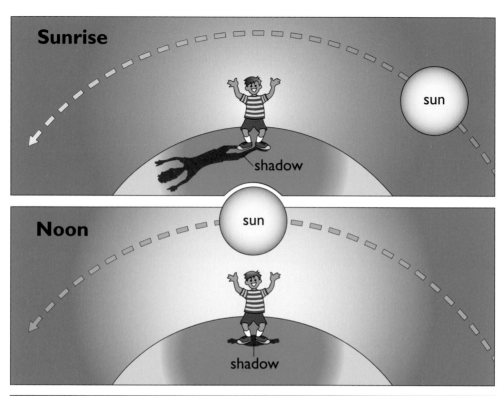

Sunrise

sun

shadow

Noon

sun

shadow

Sunset

sun

shadow

18

The Sun and Shadows

The sun stays in one place.

The earth is always spinning.

This makes it seem like the

sun moves across the sky.

When the earth spins on

a sunny day, your shadow

moves, too.

Sunny Day Facts

Without the sun, there would be no life on Earth. People, animals, and plants need the sun's heat and light to live.

The sun is the center of our solar system. Earth and all of the other planets orbit around the sun.

The sun is a medium-sized star.

The sun is a ball of hot gases.

If the sun was empty, you could fit 1,000,000 Earths in it.

The sun is about 4,500,000,000 years old.

The sun is 93,000,000 miles away. It would take you 176 years to drive there!

Never look directly at the sun! It can damage your eyes.

Glossary

 burn – to damage by the sun's rays

 melts – changes from a solid to a liquid because of heat

 shade – an area protected from the sunlight

 shadows – dark shapes made by something that is blocking the light

 skin – the outer covering on human and animal bodies

Index

The photographs in this book are reproduced through the courtesy of: © Richard Cummins, front cover, pp. 4, 5, 15, 16; © Betty Crowell, pp. 2, 7; © Norvia Behling, pp. 3, 12, 13; © Robert Fried, pp. 6, 10, 22 (2nd from top and center); © Buddy Mays/TRAVELSTOCK, pp. 8, 22 (top and bottom); © Cheryl Koenig Morgan, pp. 9, 14, 22 (2nd from bottom); © Daniel Johnson, p. 11; © Stephen Graham Photography, p. 17.

This book is available in two editions:
Library binding by Lerner Publications Company, a division of Lerner Publishing Group
Soft cover by First Avenue Editions, an imprint of Lerner Publishing Group
241 First Avenue North
Minneapolis, MN 55401 USA

Website address: www.lernerbooks.com

Library of Congress Cataloging-in-Publication Data

Nelson, Robin.
    A sunny day / by Robin Nelson.
        p.   cm. — (First step nonfiction)
    Includes index.
    ISBN 0-8225-0176-7 (lib. bdg. : alk. paper)
    ISBN 0-8225-1965-8 (pbk. : alk. paper)
    1. Sunshine—Juvenile literature. 2. Sun—Juvenile literature. [1. Sunshine. 2. Sun.] I. Title.
II. Series.
QC911.2 .N45 2002
551.5'271—dc21   00-012946

Manufactured in the United States of America
3 4 5 6 7 8 – JR – 07 06 05 04 03 02